I'm Going To READ!

CONSONANTS AND LONG VOWELS

Short Vowels

STERLING

New York / London

In this book you will learn to read these words. They have short vowels.

Short  a

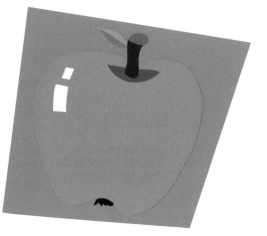

am apple bat candy cat crab
dad fan fast flag glad ham
hand hat jam mad man pan
pants ran rat sad

Short  e

bed bell belt bench desk egg
fed hen led leg let men met
nest net pen red sell shell tell
ten went wet

Short i

big chick did dig dish fill fish
kid king kiss ill lid little milk
pig pin pink ring rip ship sip
wig will zip

Short o

blocks box clock clocks dog
doll fox frog hog hop hot dog
log long mom mop pot rocks
socks song strong top

Short u

brush bug bun bus but butter
cuff cup cut drum duck fluff
fun hut jug mug nut rug run
stuff sun truck tub

Vowels

Trace and write.

cat

sun

hen

a

e

i

o

u

Consonants

Trace and write.

cat

B b

C c   D d

E f   G g

H h   J j

K k   L l

M m

N n

P p

O q

R r

S s

I t

V v

W w

X x

Y y

Z z

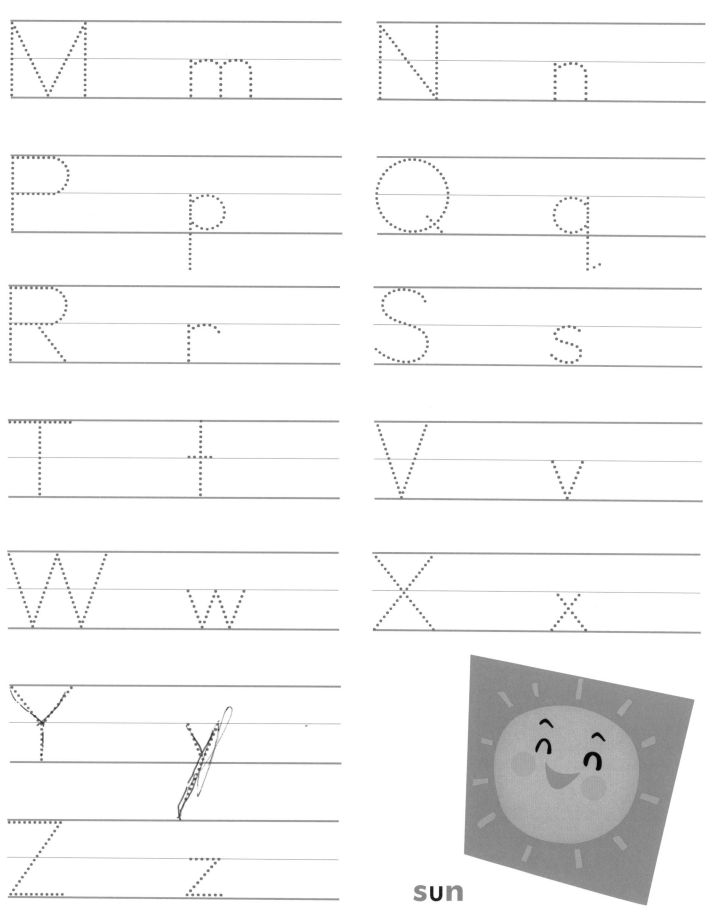

sun

Short a

rat

candy

Trace and write.

dad   **cat**   **hat**

Writing Words

Short a

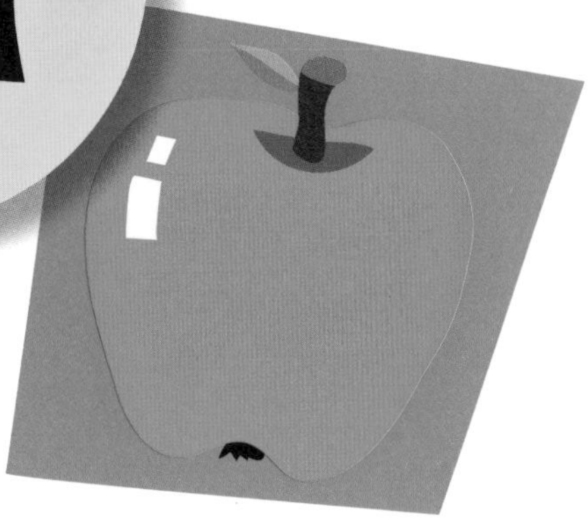

Trace and write.

apple

crab

flag

pan

candy

mad

pants

fast

hand

bat

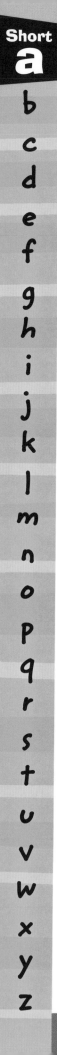

Circle all the words in each row that have a **Short**  **a** like cat.

ba**t**

tra**in**

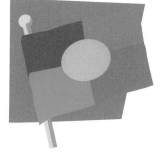

fla**g**

ca**ndy**

pla**ne**

pa**n**

ja**m**

sna**ke**

da**d**

Write the Short **a** words where they belong.

__ __ __ __ __

__ __ __

__ __ __

__ __ __ __

a
b
c
d
e
f
g
h
i
j
k
l
m
n
o
p
q
r
s
t
u
v
w
x
y
z

hat

bat

rat

cat

Rhyming Words

Write the words that rhyme with bat.

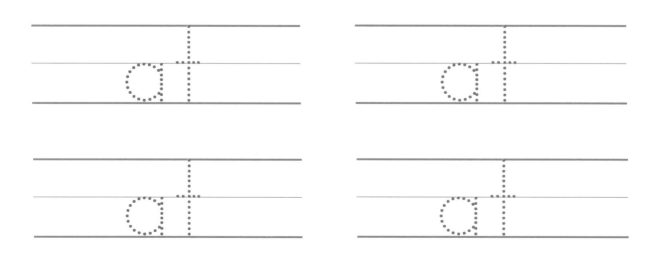

Word Endings

Read and say these words:

man	mad	ham
ban	glad	jam
fan	sad	am

Write some other words with these endings.

-an   -ad   -am

_____   _____   _____

_____   _____   _____

Can you write a rhyme?

_____

_____

_____

Short a

Fill in the missing letters to make Short **a** words.

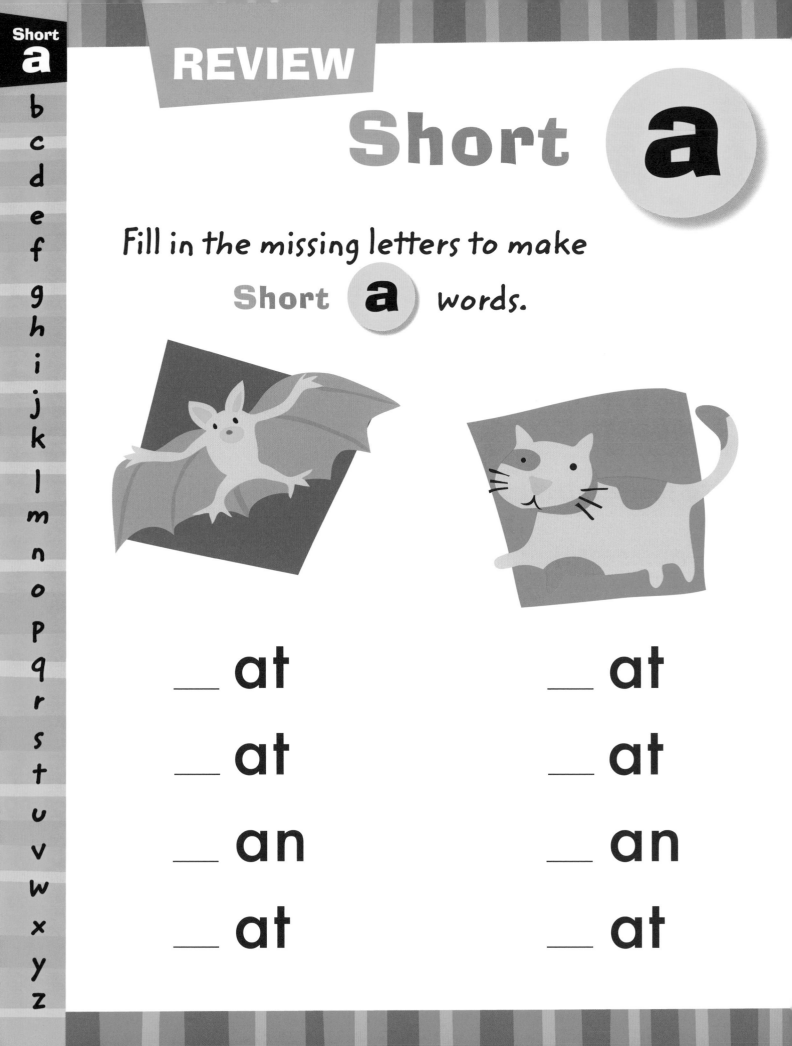

___ at

___ at

___ an

___ at

___ at

___ at

___ an

___ at

ca __

ma __

ca __

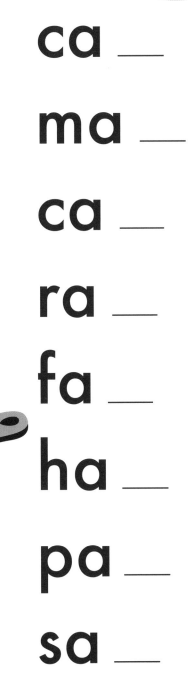

ra __

fa __

ha __

pa __

sa __

a b c d
Short
e
f g h i j k l m n o p q r s t u v w x y z

Short e

egg

hen

Trace and write.

bell

nest

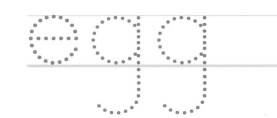

egg

nest   desk   bell

a b c d
Short
e
f g h i j k l m n o p q r s t u v w x y z

Writing Words

Short  e

Trace and write.

shell

belt

bed

net

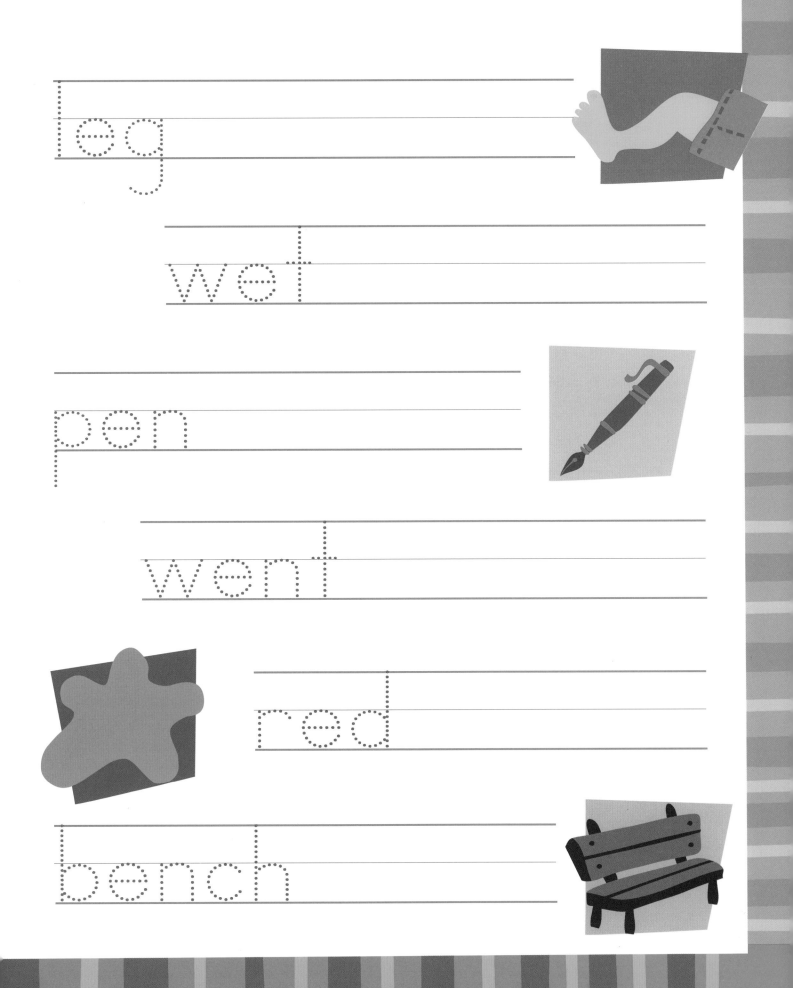

leg

wet

pen

went

red

bench

Circle all the words in each row that have a **Short e** like bed.

nest

shell

sheep

net

bee

egg

hen

belt

jeep

a b c d
Short e
f g h i j k l m n o p q r s t u v w x y z

Write the Short e words where they belong.

__ __ __ __ __ __

__ __ __

__ __ __

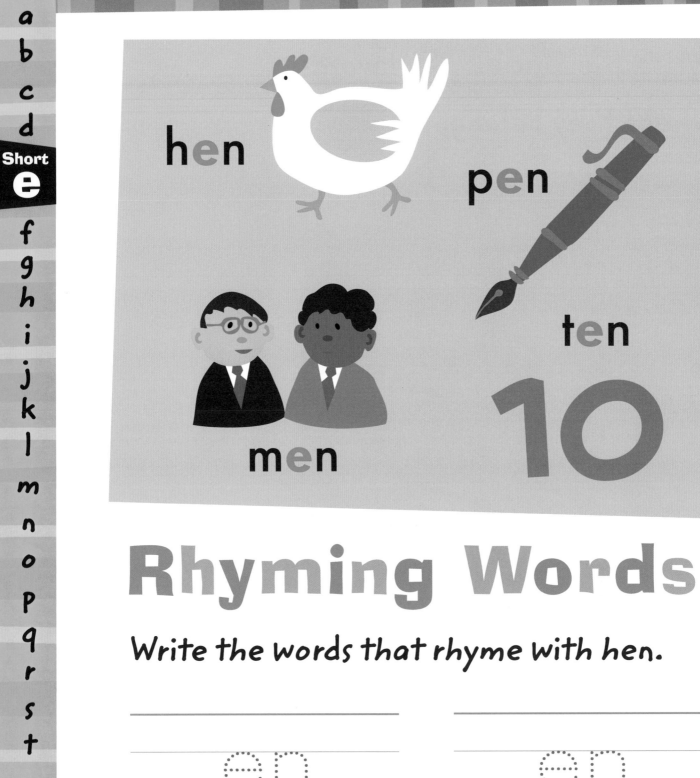

hen

pen

ten

10

men

Rhyming Words

Write the words that rhyme with hen.

en

en

en

en

Word Endings

Read and say these words:

bed	bell	net
fed	tell	let
led	sell	met

Write some other words with these endings.

-ed   -ell   -et

_____   _____   _____

_____   _____   _____

Can you write a rhyme?

_____

_____

_____

REVIEW

Short e

Fill in the missing letters to make Short **e** words.

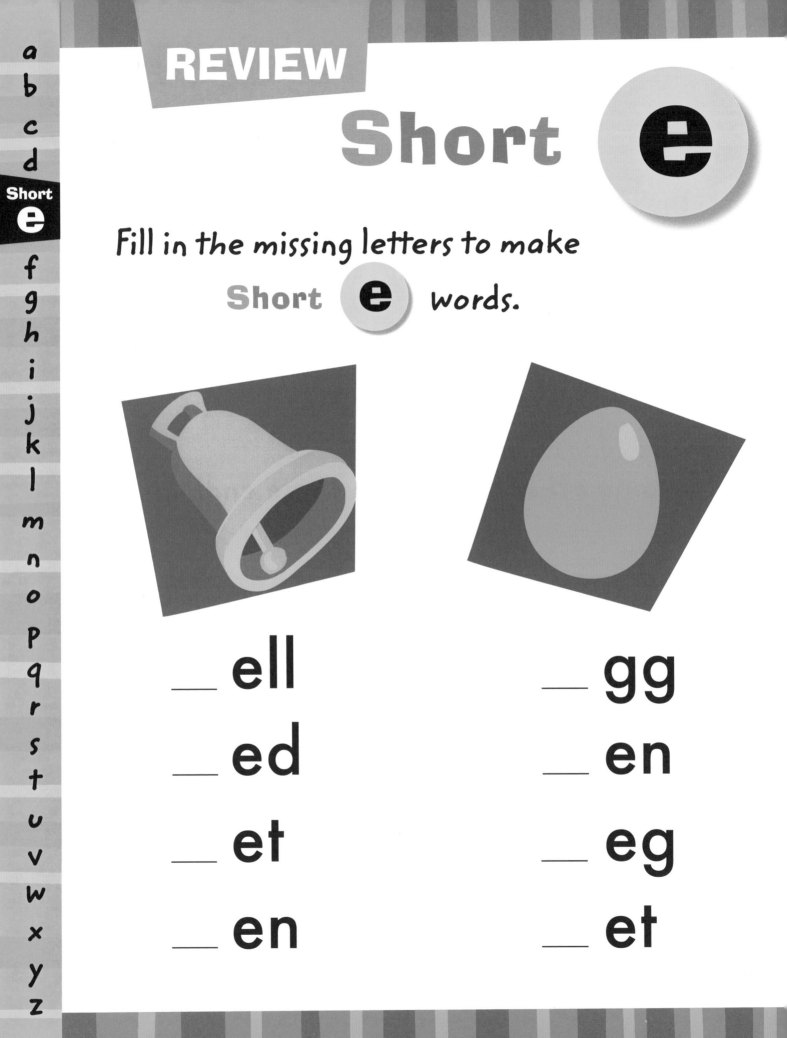

__ ell

__ ed

__ et

__ en

__ gg

__ en

__ eg

__ et

re __

be __

bel __

eg __

ne __

le __

bel __

me __

Short i

kid

pig

Trace and write.

kid

pig

pin

wig

fish   wig   pin

a b c d e f g h
Short i
j k l m n o p q r s t u v w x y z

Writing Words

Short **i**

Trace and write.

king

chick

ring

fish

ship

little

pink

kiss

milk

dish

Circle all the words in each row that have a Short **i** like pig.

milk

dish

kite

wig

bike

king

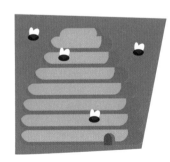

hive

fish

chick

Short i

a b c d e f g h i j k l m n o p q r s t u v w x y z

Write the Short **i** words where they belong.

_ _ _ _

_ _ _ _ _

_ _ _ _

a b c d e f g h

Short
i

j k l m n o p q r s t u v w x y z

pig

wig

big

dig

Rhyming Words

Write the words that rhyme with pig.

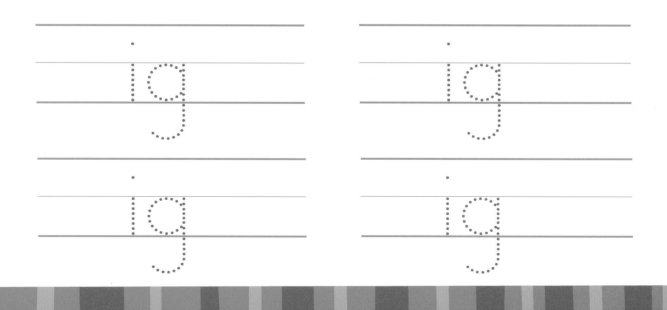

Word Endings

Read and say these words:

ill	sip	kid
will	rip	did
fill	zip	lid

Write some other words with these endings.

–ill	–ip	–id
_____	_____	_____
_____	_____	_____

Can you write a rhyme?

_____

_____

_____

Short **i**

a b c d e f g h

Short i

j k l m n o p q r s t u v w x y z

Fill in the missing letters to make
Short **i** words.

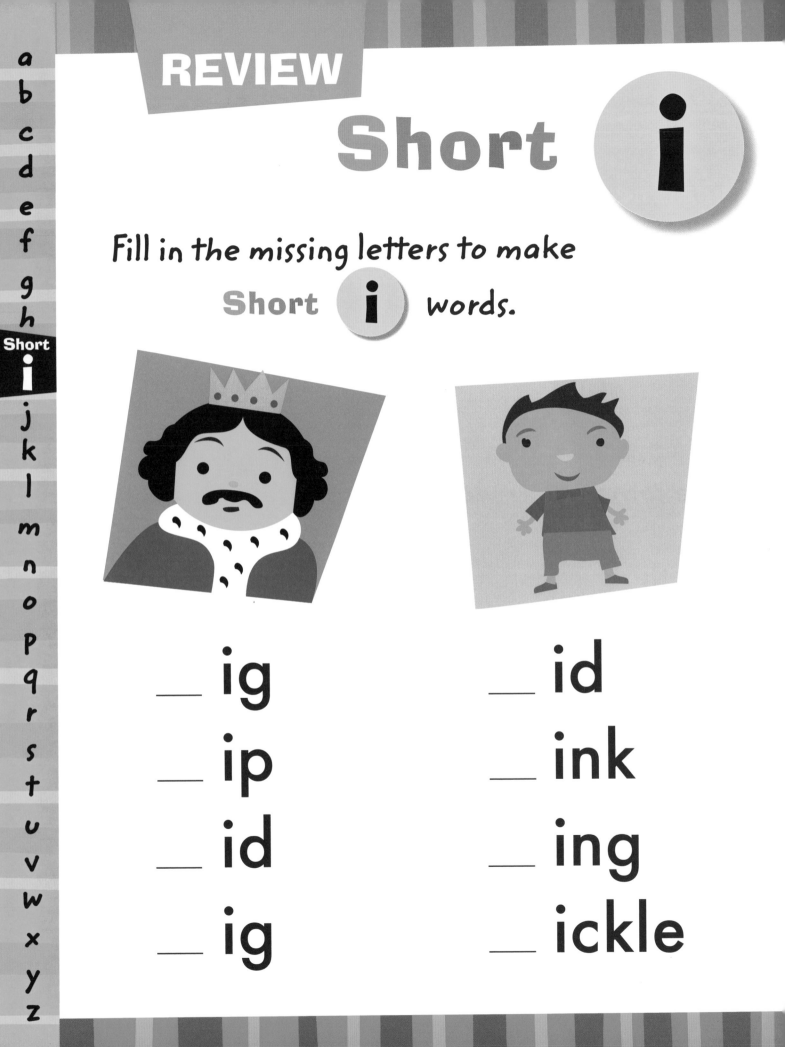

__ ig

__ ip

__ id

__ ig

__ id

__ ink

__ ing

__ ickle

pi __

pin __

si __

fis __

wi __

rin __

wis __

kis __

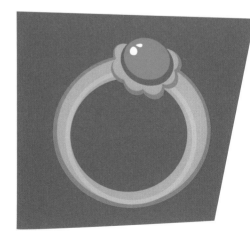

Short o

top

dog

Trace and write.

o o

dog

top

box

socks

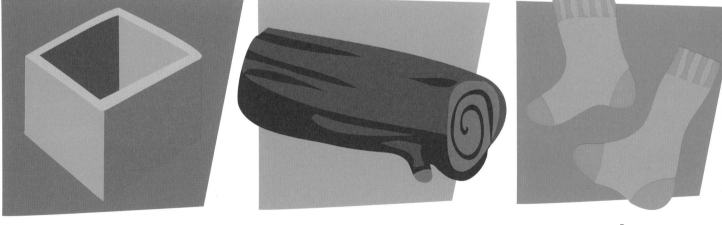

box   log   socks

Writing Words

Short o

Trace and write.

hot dog

pot

log

frog

clock

song

mom

hot

doll

fox

Circle all the words in each row that have a **Short** like frog.

d**o**ll

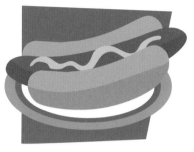

h**o**t d**o**g

pian**o**

b**o**ne

s**o**cks

d**o**g

t**o**p

p**o**t

b**o**at

Write the Short **o** words where they belong.

___ __ __ __

__ __ __ __

__ __ __

__ __ __ __ __

socks

rocks

blocks

clocks

a b c d e f g h i j k l m n o p q r s t u v w x y z

Short **o**

Rhyming Words

Write the words that rhyme with socks.

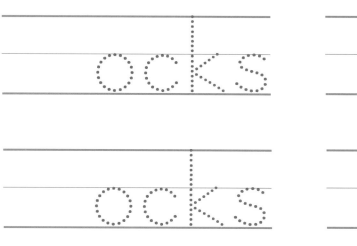

ocks

ocks

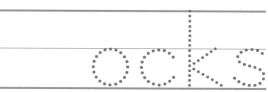

ocks

ocks

Word Endings

Read and say these words:

frog	hop	song
log	mop	long
hog	top	strong

Write some other words with these endings.

-og   -op   -ong

_____   _____   _____

_____   _____   _____

Can you write a rhyme?

_____

_____

_____

Short **o**

Fill in the missing letters to make
Short **o** words.

__og

__op

__ot

__om

__oll

__lock

__ocks

__rog

a b c d e f g h i j k l m n **Short o** p q r s t u v w x y z

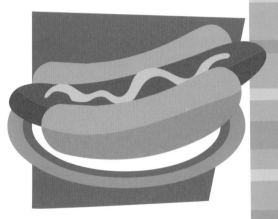

dol __

mo __

fro __

roc __

lo __

ho __

to __

son __

a b c d e f g h i j k l m n o p q r s t **Short u** v w x y z

Short U

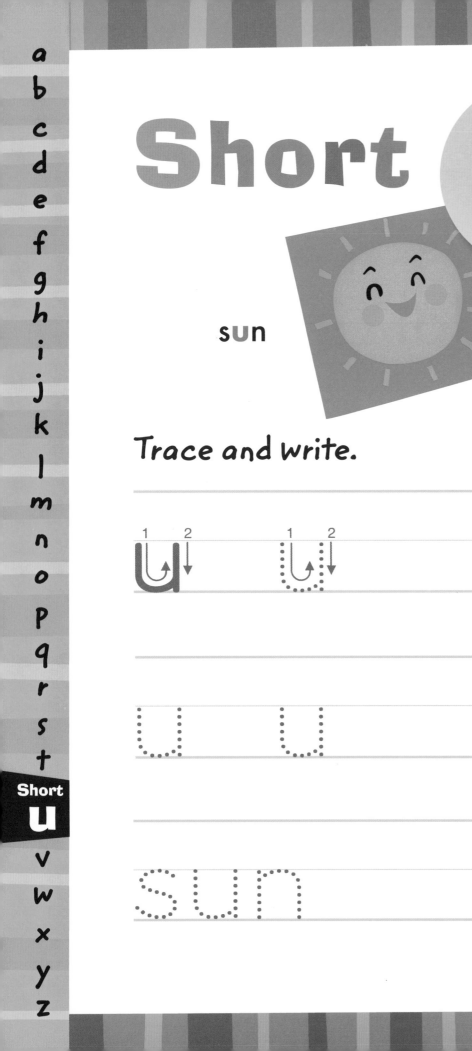

sun

bus

Trace and write.

1 2 U   1 2 U

U   U

sun

bus

bug

cup

bug

nut

cup

a b c d e f g h i j k l m n o p q r s t
u v w x y z

Writing Words
Short u

Trace and write.

truck

nut

duck

tub

drum

butter

hut

run

jug

brush

Circle all the words in each row that have a Short  like duck.

brush	truck	tuba

jug	juice	tub

sun	drum	fruit

a b c d e f g h i j k l m n o p q r s t **Short u** v w x y z

Write the **Short** **u** words where they belong.

____ __ ____ ____

____ __ ____ ____

____ __ ____ ____

____ __ ____ ____

bug

mug

rug

jug

Rhyming Words

Write the words that rhyme with bug.

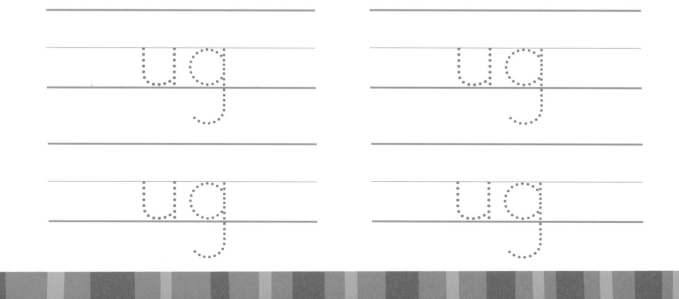

ug

ug

ug

ug

Word Endings

Read and say these words:

but	bun	cuff
cut	fun	fluff
hut	sun	stuff

Write some other words with these endings.

-ut   -un   -uff

_____   _____   _____

_____   _____   _____

Can you write a rhyme?

_____

_____

_____

Short U

Fill in the missing letters to make
Short **U** words.

__ **up**

__ **utter**

__ **ut**

__ **un**

__ **un**

__ **ub**

__ **um**

__ **p**

a b c d e f g h i j k l m n o p q r s t
Short u
v w x y z

mu __

brus __

dru __

ru __

su __

bu __

duc __

tu __

a b c d e f g h i j k l m n o p q r s t u v w x y z

REVIEW
Short Vowels

Draw a line from the word to its picture.

cat

frog

hen

fox

hot dog

candy

pig

top

kid

sun

bug

red

Short Vowels

Write the word for each picture.

Short Vowels

Say the word that goes with each picture.
If you hear a short vowel, write down the word.

a b c d e f g h i j k l m n o p q r s t u v w x y z

_____

_____

_____

_____

_____

_____

_____

_____

_____

_____

See and say:

Which words do not have short vowels?

GREAT JOB!

_____
_____
_____
date

_____
_____
first name

_____
_____
last name

★ I Can READ Short Vowels